STEM IN SPORTS:

MATH

THE STEM IN SPORTS SERIES

STEM IN SPORTS:
MATH

by James Buckley Jr.

SCIENCE TECHNOLOGY ENGINEERING MATH

Mason Crest
450 Parkway Drive, Suite D
Broomall, PA 19008
www.masoncrest.com

© 2015 by Mason Crest, an imprint of National Highlights, Inc.

Printed and bound in the United States of America.

Series ISBN: 978-1-4222-3230-9
Hardback ISBN: 978-1-4222-3232-3
EBook ISBN: 978-1-4222-8676-0

3 5 7 9 8 6 4

Produced by Shoreline Publishing Group LLC
Santa Barbara, California
Editorial Director: James Buckley Jr.
Designer: Patty Kelley
www.shorelinepublishing.com

The Library of Congress Cataloging-in-Publication Data is on
file with the publisher.

CONTENTS

KEY ICONS TO LOOK FOR:

Words to Understand: These words with their easy-to-understand definitions will increase the reader's understanding of the text, while building vocabulary skills.

Sidebars: This boxed material within the main text allows readers to build knowledge, gain insights, explore possibilities, and broaden their perspectives by weaving together additional information to provide realistic and holistic perspectives.

Research Projects: Readers are pointed toward areas of further inquiry connected to each chapter. Suggestions are provided for projects that encourage deeper research and analysis.

Text-Dependent Questions: These questions send the reader back to the text for more careful attention to the evidence presented here.

Series Glossary of Key Terms: This back-of-the-book glossary contains terminology used throughout this series. Words found here increase the reader's ability to read and comprehend higher-level books and articles in this field.

INTRODUCTION

STEM IS THE HOTTEST BUZZWORD IN education. The letters stand for Science, Technology, Engineering, and Math. Those areas of study and work will be at the forefront of business, education, careers, and life for the coming decades. More jobs are opening up in those fields than in any other areas. But as this series shows, STEM is more than just programming computers or designing new apps. The concepts of STEM cross over into just about every area of life. In this series, we focus on how STEM is impacting the world of sports.

This volume focuses on Mathematics. Sports is packed with numbers, of course. Math is fundamental to nearly every sport.

How else can you tell who won without comparing the numbers, whether points, yards, wins, shots, or distances? You've got uniform numbers and game scores and player statistics. Then you have the huge dollar figures in pro sports, or even ticket sales and attendance. But in recent years, math has begun to play an even bigger role in sports. New ideas about gathering and using data and plugging that data into formulas have transformed how athletes, teams, and fans interact with their sports and games. What we hope to do here is not to shower you with formulas and homework, but to inspire you to look at ways that numbers can make your love of sports (and maybe your skill with sports) grow.

CHAPTER 1

ATHLETES PLAY

The first numbers most sports fans deal with are the ones that the players wear. After that, it gets complicated.

IN MOST TEAM SPORTS, PLAYERS START AS SIMPLY A number: that is, the number they wear on their jersey. But athletes today go way beyond just using their math knowledge to make sure they're wearing the right number. For athletes, math can be something they do on purpose to help their game: tracking their stats or using data to learn how they're improving. Math can also affect players without them really knowing it. Math formulas can describe actions on the field in ways that experts can use to improve those actions. However, an athlete who looks at the math (and physics) behind his or her actions can get a running start on the competition.

Uniform Numbers

HERE'S AN OLD SAYING IN BASEBALL: YOU CAN'T tell the players without a scorecard. That's because when baseball began using uniform numbers (in the 1920s, believe it or not), the players did not have their names on the back, as most do today. So you needed a list of numbers in the scorecard to match the numbers with the names.

Like numbers in many walks of life, uniform numbers in sports can tell stories. The first baseball jersey numbers were assigned to a player's spot in the batting order. That's why the great Babe Ruth wore number 3 and Lou Gehrig wore number 4. Guess where they batted in the New York Yankees' lineup? Of course, that tradition fell aside as teams used more and more players and did not always use a set lineup day after day. Today, baseball players have numbers up and down the scale, though most top out in the 30s. If you see a player with a uniform in the 60s or 70s, chances are he is a short-term rookie. A few players have chosen to wear big numbers, such as the Dodgers' Hyun-jin Ryu, who sports number 99.

In soccer, the jersey (or "kit," to use the English term) numbers first came from positions on the field. Until the mid-1960s, subs were not allowed in top-flight soccer. So the 11 players who started were the 11 who finished. The goalies were assigned number 1,

the defenders 2 through 5, the midfielders 6 through 8, and the forwards 9 through 11. Even today, though the numbers now range much wider, the number 10 jersey is expected to be worn by a team's top scorer. Famous number 10s have included Brazil's Péle, Italy's Roberto Baggio and Francesco Totti, and France's Zinedine Zidane. Of course, one number 10 player is a man most call the best in the world today (and winner of the Golden Ball at the 2014 World Cup) Argentina's Lionel Messi.

In many sports, uniform numbers take on mythical proportions because of who wore them. The Pittsburgh Pirates' great Roberto

The No. 10 jersey marks Messi as Argentina's "go-to" player . . . though by now most people don't need a number to know his greatness.

Lou Gehrig's number 4 was the first jersey ever retired. Babe Ruth (3) and Joe DiMaggio (5) followed, the first of the Yankees' MLB-record 17 retired jeseys.

Clemente wore number 21. In 2013, when the Pirates made the playoffs, manager Clint Hurdle knew that one of the driving forces for the team that year was to end their playoff drought at 20 years. Before the season began, he told the Clemente family that he didn't want the team to have 21 straight losing seasons because it might affect the legend of Clemente's 21.

Legendary players often have their numbers retired; that is, no one from that team can ever wear it again. The New York Yankees have retired 17 numbers, the most of any baseball team. In the NBA, the Boston Celtics have put 21 numbers out of commission. The most famous retired number is 42. That was worn by Jackie Robinson, who in 1947 became the first African-American player in the Majors in the 20th century. In 1997, on the 50th anniversary of his appearance, Major League Baseball retired number 42 for all teams for all time, showing clearly how a number can become a symbol.

Stats, of Course

PLAYERS WEAR NUMBERS ON THEIR BACKS, BUT THEY make numbers on the field. Statistics are the lifeblood of most sports. Statistics is actually a complete branch of higher mathematics, studied in upper high school and college. The techniques used in those studies have migrated into sports in new and amazing ways. We'll look at some of them in each chapter, as stats have different applications for each part of the sports world.

For athletes, stats are a way to measure their success. They track how they're doing just as fans and team owners and managers are doing. But for players, those stats are more personal. They don't need to get involved in the higher math of calculating obscure new stats (see page 25). They focus on the stats that drive their success: points, speed, time, distance, etc.

Track-and-field athletes aim for PRs: personal records. They can see how much they have improved each time they set a new best in a sprint, jump, or throw. They can look at specific parts of their training to see how they can make the next PR . . . and the next.

Golfers track a similar type of score. They are not affected by any teammates or opponents. It's just them against the course. If they can see their scoring numbers tracking lower (of course, in golf, the low score wins),

Oh, So Close

Statistics in the "counting" stats are easy to measure. Count up the hits, goals, strikeouts, free throws, races won, etc. and you see who has the most. In categories that use averages, however, the answers are not always as clear.

In 2003, for example, the National League batting average title needed four decimal places to find a winner. (Batting average is figured by dividing the number of hits a player has by the number of official at-bats. A player with a .300 average, or about 3 hits in every 10 AB, is considered very good.) That year, Albert Pujols of the St. Louis Cardinals hit .35871, while Todd Helton of the Colorado Rockies ended at .35849. It was the closest in N.L. history,

In the NBA, there have been several similar races for the league's high scorer. The title goes to the player with the highest average per game. In 2013, Carmelo Anthony of the New York Knicks squeaked ahead of the Oklahoma City Thunder's Kevin Durant, 28.7 to 28.1. The closest ever, though, came in 1978, when George Gervin of the Spurs edged out David Thompson of the Nuggets, 27.22 to 27.15. Gervin had to score 63 points in the final game to nab the crown.

they know they are improving. Golf also can break down the total score very easily into drives, irons, and putts. A player knows that fewer putts means a lower score, so counting those in a round is a quick way to gauge improvement.

Team sports athletes look at their individual achievements, but for the most part understand that those are accomplished with the help of others. A basketball player can try to improve his scoring, but only if his teammates get him the ball. A football player wants to score more points, but can only reach the end zone with good blocking.

Players in all sports use stats to compare to players past and present. By creating a set of measurements that remain constant over time, an athlete in 2015 can look at an athlete in 1965 or 1915 and compare the numbers.

Golf is the rare sport in which a lower score is a better score.

Having an understanding of stats is part of being an athlete. But all the numbers in the world won't help once the game starts. Then math goes away and physics, in the form of effort, energy, and skill, takes over.

Moving the Ball

ATHLETES IN MANY SPORTS PROBABLY DON'T KNOW it, but they're using the math of physics whenever they play. Let's look at some examples of how math can help players (and fans) understand an athlete's skills. And remember, geometry is a branch of math.

David Beckham became world famous for his ability to "bend" the soccer ball. He didn't bend the ball, of course; it remained a perfect sphere. What he bent was its flight. Scientists studied his amazing skills and came to some conclusions: It was physics and math in action. By doing specific physical things in the right proportions, Beckham and, of course,

Beckham (23) shows off his physics-based ball-bending skills.

other great soccer-ball kickers plug them-selves into a mathematical formula that turns numbers into action. In 2012, some English physics students even wrote this formula down (below). Without getting too deep, what it basically says is that you can figure out how much a ball will bend (D) if you know the size (R) and weight (m) of the ball, the **velocity** (or speed: v) it is traveling, the density of the air (p), and how far it is being kicked (x).

$$D = \frac{\pi R^3 pw}{vm} X^2$$

Bowling balls are another type of sphere that athletes can make move in mysterious ways. In bowling, you've got a hard sphere touching a hard, oiled surface at one point at all times. A bowler makes the ball spin in such a way that the momentum of the spin forces the mass of the ball to make a specific turn. An expert bowler can also take into account the friction created by different types of lane oiling. With practice (and the hidden forces of math and physics), a bowler can create a predictable spin that he or she can change de-pending on what they're aiming at.

Cricket bowlers combine a bit of base-ball with a bit of trickery. The only math fast bowlers need shows the miles per hour their deliveries are moving. Like baseball pitch-

When the ball leaves this shooter's hands, it should be moving along a 50.8 degree angle for the best chance of success.

ers, faster usually means better. The other major type of cricket bowler, however, is called a spin bowler. By using the seam of the ball and the twists of his wrist, the spin bowler can make a round ball move in very interesting ways. Again, physics and math describe these rotations as formulas that combine weight, speed, and angle. Bowlers, like a great curveball pitcher in baseball, are using math in every game without knowing it!

Basketball is an activity that probably doesn't look like it needs math, but there is a lot of geometry, especially in the art of shooting. For a shot to go into the basket, it needs to follow the right path, or arc, from the shooter's hand to the rim. Use the right arc, two points. Use the wrong one, clang! A player doesn't need to know the perfect angle at which her elbow should be or the arc the shot should follow. But by understanding how that affects success, she can improve her game tremendously. In fact, studies that look at different angles and techniques have actually come up with an answer: It depends!

Actually, that answer makes sense if you look at the math. To create the proper arc to take a ball from point A to point B, you need to know the starting point A. And that point will differ because players are different heights. One chart put together by a physics professor broke it down by those various heights. On the chart, a six-foot (1.82 m) player should shoot at a 50.8-degree angle. A shorter player, 5 feet 4 inches (1.65 m), needs to aim at 52.2 degrees. A very tall, seven-foot (2.13 m) player has a lesser angle of 48.7 degrees. Athletes, of course, don't have time to calculate angles every time they shoot. (Try pulling out a protractor with someone's hand in your face and the shot clock running down!) But by understanding the perfect angles, practice can make hitting the right number as easy as hitting the right shot.

TEXT-DEPENDENT QUESTIONS

1. What does it mean to "retire" a number?
2. What science helps determine how David Beckham bends a soccer ball?
3. Why do basketball players need to know about arcs?

RESEARCH PROJECTS

Pick three track-and-field running distances. Then have someone time you running those events. Then see if you can train to set a new PR in each. The numbers will tell the story of your success!

CHAPTER 2

FANS LEAD THE WAY

An avalanche of data and information has transformed the way that fans watch and understand sports.

S O, SPORTS ARE PACKED WITH NUMBERS, FROM uniforms to physics formulas to shooting arcs. But that was not enough for many people. In the early part of the 2000s, thousands of fans began to use the power of the Internet—with its ability to find and gather huge amounts of material—to dig even deeper into the sports they loved. What they discovered is that the old ways of looking at math and sports were too limited, too small. The idea was that by having huge amounts of information—or "big data," as it has come to be called—to sift through, they could gain more knowledge by looking at just a little bit of information.

People began to see that what had been "wisdom" in sports was not based on actual data, but more on memories or "gut feelings." It was one thing for a coach to say that a player might do better in a given situation. It was another thing entirely to show mathematically that a player would . . . or would not. In statistics, the concept is known as a "sample size" problem. If you have knowledge of something happening 10 times, you can then see if something happens only 10 percent of the time—1 out of 10 being the lowest you can see (other than zero, of course). But if you can look at 1,000 or 100,000 times that something happens, you can get closer and closer, mathematically, to a more certain answer. That's the power of big data, and that power is changing how we look at sports.

Sabermetrics

BASEBALL HAS LONG BEEN THE STARTING POINT WHEN talking about sports and math. Every play in a game adds a string of digits to a dozen or more categories, and every inning adds more, while every game generates page after page of stats, averages, situations, results, and possibilities. Old-time baseball people used to complain that stats could tell a manager which hitters would perform best on Wednesdays in June against a left-handed pitcher whose last name had six or more let-

ters, or some other combination of choices. Thanks to an obsessive collection of people who record every possible event in every Major League game, making a choice like that—and perhaps even more obscure—is now child's play.

Though analyzing stats in baseball has probably been around since the day after the first games were played, in-depth charting of this info really gained notice in the 1980s and 1990s. One of the prime movers was a man named Bill James, who created an annual photocopied journal packed with stats-based analysis. He did most of his work during

One pitch turns into a stack of stats, from location to type of pitch to batter's average and more. And then it starts again with the next pitch.

boring nights while working as a night watchman. James was a member of the Society for American Baseball Research (SABR, pronounced "SAY-ber") and he came up with the name "Sabermetrics" to describe his type of stats work. Over time, James's work spread deeper and deeper into the baseball stat community.

In the mid-1990s, the creation of the Internet signaled a huge leap forward in applying the work of James and others. The Internet has put complete play-by-play and pitch-by-pitch information for just about every game ever played online. Using endlessly entertaining formulas (see box for some examples), Sabermetricians (that is, people using Sabermetrics) filled pages and pages of Web sites with deep analysis using existing baseball stats.

Some fans and teams stick with the old-fashioned methods of score-keeping on paper, but that process generates numbers, too.

They were not all full-time analysts. Most were everyday fans with not-so-everyday knowledge of high-end statistics, computer analysis, and research expertise. However, in the years that followed, it became easier and

The SABR World of Stats

With the growth of Sabermetrics, baseball added a whole new pile of stats to its already-large inventory. Here are a few of the most well-known with a short explanation of how they are calculated.

OPS: On-base Percentage + Slugging Average

By combining a stat that shows how often a player reaches base with a stat that shows his extra-base power, OPS has come to be more valued than batting average among baseball experts.

WAR: Wins Above Replacement

This stat combines some simple and some obscure stats to answer the question: How many wins a season is a player worth to his team than the league-average replacement for his spot? The all-time leader in WAR for a career is no surprise: Babe Ruth at 183.6. For a modern-day leader, look at the Angels' Mike Trout, who led the American League in 2012, 2013, and 2014. His highest total was 10.9 WAR in 2012.

BABIP: Batting Average of Balls Hit Into Play

This takes strikeouts out of the hitting equation by only looking at how successful a player is when he actually hits the ball fair. The 2014 leader was Kansas City outfielder Lorenzo Cain at .373, 75 points above his regular batting average. Want to find your own BABIP? Use this formula:

$$\text{BABIP} = \frac{\text{Hits} - \text{Home runs}}{\text{At-bats} - \text{Strikeouts} - \text{Home runs} + \text{Sacrifice Flies}}$$

UZR: Ultimate Zone Rating

Fielding in baseball has always been hard to put a number on. Fielding average (errors per fielding chance) has never really been enough. Sabermetrics came up with several new stats, with UZR gaining a lot of use. It combines several stats into one to create a single number that can be compared among all fielders or among fielders at each position. The idea is to come up with how many runs a player's defensive skills saved his team. In 2014, third baseman Chase Headley (Padres/Yankees) led the way with a UZR of 20.9.

easier to join this revolution.

In 2013, in fact, Colin Wyers, the director of operations for Baseball Prospectus (a leading Sabermetric Web site), told writer Jack Moore that "the honest truth is, it has never been easier to be a sabermetrician than it is right now. You can go into any Wal-Mart in the country and pick up an absurdly powerful personal computer for a few hundred dollars. You get that thing home and hook it up to [the] Internet and you can download large amounts of rich, rich baseball data for free."

Eventually, not even the tradition-based leaders of baseball could ignore this revolution. But we'll see how they reacted in the next chapter.

Math Lovers Unite!

THE GROWTH IN INTEREST AMONG FANS—AND among sports professionals—in statistical analysis created a need for them to gather to find out more. Numerous conferences are held every year at which amateurs and pros alike present a bewildering list of speeches and papers on deeply obscure topics. They use math formulas like a pitcher uses a curveball or a golfer wields a putter. The most well-known is the MIT (Massachusetts Institute of Technology) Sloan Sports **Analytics** Conference. It has been held since 2007 and has gotten bigger every year. It at-

tracts the biggest names in sports. In 2014, for example, NBA Commissioner Adam Silver spoke on one panel, Sabermetrics founder Bill James gave a talk, and executives from a dozen top pro sports teams shared their expertise.

Baseball is the leading topic for many such conferences. Here are some of the presentation topics at the 2014 MIT event:

- Beyond Pythagorean Expectation: How Run Distributions Affect Win Percentage
- Workforce Analytics in Baseball Player Management
- Putting the D [for Defense] in Data

But it's not just baseball. Other Sloan presentations included ones on "Hidden Field

New England Patriots president Jonathan Kraft, moderator Jackie MacMullan, and New York Knicks president Phil Jackson spoke about building dynasties at the 2014 Sloan event.

Vision in English Premier League Soccer," "An Improved Plus-minus Statistic for the NHL," and "Fightnomics: What really matters in professional fighting."

From the keynote speaker to the final question-and-answer period, everyone involved in these conferences knows that the power of mathematics, using the energy of big data, can transform how we think about, understand, and organize sports at every level.

Fantasy Sports and Math

WHILE THE PEOPLE AT THE MIT CONFERENCE and others look at math in the real world, millions of fans look at math in a fantasy way. Fantasy sports is almost literally nothing but sports and math. In fantasy sports, a person chooses a team of real-life players in a particular sport. Then that person's "fantasy" team gains points and competes against other fantasy players based on the real-life results of those players. Team owners can draft, cut, trade, and research players, just like sports team executives in real life. It almost does not matter who wins or loses a game, as long as your players get their points for "your" team. And there are fantasy leagues for just about every sport you can think of, from baseball and football to cricket and Formula 1, from hockey to golf.

No matter what fantasy sport you play,

knowing the math is key to succeeding. Every type of league counts points in its own way. Fantasy football is the most popular of the sports; NFL.com reports that more than 40 million people played some sort of fantasy sport in 2013. In most fantasy football leagues, you play head-to-head each week against another fantasy team. Knowing how your league counts points is the key to setting up a winning team. How many points does your quarterback get for a touchdown pass? What running backs will score the most points in both rushing and receiving? Which team has an offense that leads to long field goals? The answers to all of those are found by understanding the numbers and reading the stats. So the next time math class seems boring, remember that you can't win in sports—fantasy or reality—without knowing the numbers.

Some fans root for the Colts. Many others root for Andrew Luck when he plays for their fantasy football teams.

Gambling

FANTASY SPORTS IS A KIND OF GAMBLING ON SPORTS, but only a very few people make a living at it or try to win a lot of money. For

As shown on the board in the background, horseracing is awash in numbers, odds, bets, and times.

the vast majority of people, fantasy sports mostly is a game for fun. Money is not the object. For another area of sports that depends on math, winning money is the only object. Sports gambling is a multi-billion-dollar industry in the United States, though it can be legally done only in Nevada. But fans flock by the millions to casinos there to place bets on just about every kind of sporting event.

When doing so, they are using math at every turn. The most obvious is the point spread. In most sports, the casino determines by how many points a team is "favored" over another; that is, the spread is how many points the casino thinks a team will win by. A fan placing a bet on the favorite only wins his bet if his team wins by more than that set number of points. Bettors need to understand this key math before they risk their money. Other bets are taken on the total points scored in the game or even a halftime score. For many fans, the reality of sports gambling is a far more important part of sports than the fantasy of owning their own team.

Fans always know who won or lost a game. In recent years, using math, stats, and analysis, they have helped the sports world learn a lot more than that.

TEXT-DEPENDENT QUESTIONS

1. Who was one the most important figures in the history of "Sabermetrics"?
2. Where is the famous Sloan Sports Analytics Conference held?
3. Why do fantasy sports players need to know math?

RESEARCH PROJECTS

It's not homework . . . it's practice! Use the BABIP formula on page 25 and find out how your favorite players did in their most recent full season. A great place to get the raw materials for the equation is www.baseball-reference.com.

LEADERBOARD

1	M ILONEN	-18	0
2	A NOREN	-16	0
3	J BLIXT	-14	0
3	M MANASSERO	-14	0
5	R KARLBERG	-12	0
6	B WIESBERGER	-11	0
6	J LUITEN	-11	0
6	T BJÖRN	-11	0
9	J QUESNE	-10	0
9	P LARRAZABAL	-10	0

CHAPTER 3

TEAMS & LEAGUES FOLLOW

WHILE FANS STARTED THE REVOLUTION IN statistical analysis, teams and leagues quickly realized that they had to catch up. They needed to do so as part of their business. In the past decade, the use of advanced math and statistics has skyrocketed inside team and league offices. The "old" methods of just counting hits or tracking simple averages are no longer enough. Using the power of computing and the creativity of experts (and calling on the expertise of those everyday fans with new ideas), numbers in sports have gotten even more important. From the boardroom when drafting contracts, to the draft room when pick-

This golf leaderboard shows how basic sports math can be. But that is just the starting point for sports today.

ing **prospects,** to the locker room when making lineups, advanced stats and math are now as much a part of sports as sweat and matching uniforms.

The New Numbers Guys

SABERMETRICS WAS STILL A RELATIVELY NEW PHEnomenon when Oakland Athletics general manager Billy Beane got to work in 1997. Beane, a former big-league player, realized earlier than most executives that diving deep into the numbers could really help him choose players. His approach broke some of the baseball "rules" and he was able to put together a team of players that many other teams had rejected. The author Michael Lewis, who normally reported on financial matters, followed the A's and wrote the book *Moneyball* in 2003 about Beane's methods. The book was a huge hit and exposed to a much wider audience the ideas behind Sabermetrics and advanced analysis in baseball. A movie based on the book and starring Brad Pitt helped make the story even bigger.

After seeing the A's success, other baseball teams (and even teams in other sports) began to look at the sort of math-based and analysis-based decision-making Beane was using. Bill James was hired by the Boston Red Sox in 2002. James had set the standard for big-data based analysis, and it opened the

WORDS TO UNDERSTAND

dynamic pricing a system of changing the price of an event or a product based on calculations showing the seller how to get the best price

logistics the process of organizing large amounts of goods, events, or people over a set period of time

prospects young athletes being looked at as future pro players

STEM IN SPORTS: MATH

floodgates. Team after team looked around the tech world or at Ivy League math majors to find people who could provide the computer-savvy, stats-oriented analysis that would help their teams win.

In 2012, for example, the Houston Astros went all-in on analytics. They hired Sig Mejdal as the vice president of decision sciences. What sounds like something from a sci-fi movie is now a part of America's National Pastime. Mejdal describes his job as "maximizing your output in an uncertain world. That's our job: Creating decision aids based on the analysis in order to assist our decision

Thanks to the Athletics stat- and data-based player development, they had a lot of high-fives during a very successful 2014 season.

Whether this went for two or three points, it's now part of the statistical record NBA teams are using to judge and choose players.

makers." Wow, that's a mouthful, but what it means is that Mejdal and others like him provide the bosses with the numbers they need to decide.

It's not just baseball, either. In 2014, hockey's Edmonton Oilers hired Tyler Dellow to work in their front office. Dellow made his name writing a blog that analyzed hockey stats in the same thoughtful, big-data way that Sabermetricians do in baseball. The New Jersey Devils, Nashville Predators, and Toronto Maple Leafs also hired people, most described by SI.com as "youngsters," to beef up their stats analysis. More than 15 NBA teams now have full-time sports stat analysts, bringing math to a sport that used to only worry about points and assists. In fact, the Milwaukee Bucks' Michael Clutterbuck is one of several people who have the title of Director of Basketball Analytics.

The concept of using stats and math in deeper ways started outside the main pro sports. Fans proved that it worked, and teams have followed their lead. The outsiders have become the insiders.

Using Stats to Draft

It's one thing for fans to enjoy looking at stats. It's another when those fans invade the team offices, calculators in hand. But that happened in 2014, when the NBA's Sacramento Kings invited fans to help them make their draft picks.

The team had a contest to find fans with deep stats knowledge. They announced the Draft 3.0 Challenge and invited fans to submit ideas on how they would use advanced stat analysis to find players that would fit the Kings' needs.

"There is so much talent and so much information out there today outside of the walls of the NBA," said Kings' general manager Pete D'Alessandro. "I felt like we could tap into that vast wealth of knowledge." In the end, the Kings asked five members of the public—including businessmen and college students—to attend the draft and chip in their points of view. It turned out that both the stat guys and the team scouts liked the same player, forward Nik Stauskas of Michigan. And so the Kings made him their first-round pick.

Like the Moneyball discussion of scouts versus stats, the Kings looked to both camps for answers. "We all like to hear a confident answer," said D'Alessandro. "I like to give confident answers but also in my mind see something in black-and-white that helps me support that answer. I think it's just my nature. So having a group like that to help support the eye-test of my scouts was really good."

"Mathematics have been very influential to our decision-making process for our team," said Eugene Martinez, one of the contest winners. "We wanted to look at the cultural fit for the different prospects, but we [also] wanted to look at the statistics from the collegiate level that each of the players brought to the team. Where are the trends?"

For smart sports executives, the answer is not black or white. It's not a choice between

Fan analysts and Sacramento experts agreed that Michigan's Stauskas was worth a first-round selection.

STEM IN SPORTS: MATH

something to drink or something to eat. When using numbers to evaluate players, whether those numbers are simple or complex, the choice is easy: Use both numbers and "eyes." Eat *and* drink. A computer can't pick a whole team, but a scout can't know all the answers without checking the stats.

Numbers in Football

BASEBALL IS NOT THE ONLY SPORT LOOKING FOR deeper meaning in the numbers. Football has jumped into the data game with both cleats. And it's not just the big yard-line numbers that cover the field.

Outside experts have been drafted to help

Football is not being left behind in the race to mine data. A hit like this one will generate a stack of useful stats.

NFL and college football teams dive into the numbers. The Football Outsiders web site packs its pages with endless charts, stats, graphs, and more, all culled from huge lists of stats and numbers. They are so obsessive that they even correct the "official" stats sometimes. In one instance noted on ESPN.com, Football Outsiders found that 30 percent of plays run at home by the San Diego Chargers were from a no-huddle offense. The official stadium stats didn't note the difference between huddle or no-huddle plays. A team looking at the Chargers as a future opponent needs to know about those no-huddle plays, so looking for help outside official channels could pay off.

Other big areas of football stats knowledge that teams use include analysis of the chances for success on third- and fourth-down plays. The traditional coaches will rarely "go for it" on fourth down, usually choosing to punt. Analysis of the various situations shows that trying for a first down in many fourth-down situations is, over the long

To punt or not to punt: That is the question that analysts are trying to answer using stats rather than "guts."

Capologists

Several major pro sports leagues place a salary cap on their teams. That is, a team cannot spend more than X amount of dollars on salaries per season. That helps to level the playing field and not let one team simply outspend the others. With the creation of those caps, a new type of job emerged: the capologist.

These executives need to have a great knowledge of math and accounting to be able to track and calculate salaries, bonuses, and long-term contracts. They also have to be experts in their sport, as well as understand their team's needs and goals. It's a juggling act that has become a vital part of many teams' front offices in the NFL, NHL, and NBA. One capologist explains how it works in his sport.

"In hockey, if you only base your analysis on goals, you're going to miss 98 percent of the other things that are happening that have value," Frank Provenzano of the National Hockey League's Dallas Stars told the *Globe & Mail*. "So what are those things, and what value do they have, and then how do you translate that value into your decision making—into dollars."

It's the capologist's job to tell his bosses how many of those dollars a player is worth . . . and whether they have room for that player "under the cap."

term, statistically positive. But here is where the debate between mind and math comes in: Most coaches still trust their guts, which tell them to punt and try later, even if the math says to take a chance.

Another area math is used is in deciding when to go for a two-point conversion after a touchdown. Most coaches have memorized or carry with them a chart that shows the different situations that come up in a game. Simply following the math on the chart gives the coach the best chance for success. For example, the chart might say that a team trailing by 2 or 5 points in the fourth quarter should go for two. A team behind by 3, 6, 7, or 8 should kick the extra point instead. Stopping the game to work that out in his head would cost a coach his job, so it's a good thing the math has been done for him!

A simple chart of numbers shows football coaches whether to kick an extra point or "go for two."

Math and Tickets

HOW MUCH SHOULD YOU CHARGE FOR TICKETS TO your team's game? That is no longer a simple question for pro team executives. They have turned to math for some answers. And they've also figured out how to make money in the process. The buzzword is **dynamic pricing**. That means that teams adjust the prices of their game tickets based on the opponent, time of the year, or even importance of the game. It's no longer a guessing game: Math tells the teams what the market will bear.

The Los Angeles Dodgers are one of several teams that use mathematical formulas, combined with a little marketing knowledge, to create "tiers" of games and ticket prices. That is, they look at their schedule and figure out which games will be more popular with fans. Then they can charge more for those games, knowing from their data that fans will pay more for those more popular games.

Russ Stanley of the San Francisco Giants told Forbes.com, "All games are not created equal. We have seen an increase of seven percent [in ticket revenue] in the back-to-back years we implemented dynamic pricing. We have also been able to sell more tickets to lesser games because we can follow what the market will bear and accurately price tickets."

Some teams in the NBA and NHL use dynamic pricing, too. The Orlando Magic goes another step, using analytics to look at season ticket sales. They watch fan buying behavior and analyze numbers of all sorts to make sure that the offers they make season-ticket fans are the ones that fans want. After doing all that work, the Magic claims to have the seventh-best revenue from tickets in the NBA . . . in a market that is 20th-largest in the league. Math is helping turns fan "likes" into dollars for the Magic.

Math Makes Opening Day

THANK GOODNESS FOR MATH AND COMPUTERS. That is the only way to make 32 NFL teams, their owners, and their fans happy. Well, almost. Making a schedule for a professional league is a case study in the science of **logistics**, which uses math, graphs, spreadsheets, and calendars to solve problems of space and time.

For decades, the NFL schedule was made by a man named Val Pinchbeck, who used paper and pencil and a big board with hanging, movable tags. More recently, computers have done the hard work of churning through more than 500,000 possible schedules to arrive at the one that works. Four NFL employees, however, program that computer to make sure that TV networks, players, coaches, and stadiums all get—nearly—what they want. The human side of this equation has to understand the needs of TV to get good games. But they also have to tell the computer when One Direction is playing at a stadium or when another stadium might have a rugby game the day before (leaving a beat-up field for Sunday!). They have to tell the computer to avoid having West Coast teams make back-

Dynamic pricing and mining of fan data helped the Magic pack the Amway Arena.

to-back cross-country flights. And dozens of other variables that have to be considered.

Major League Baseball depended on a very patient and organized couple named the Stephensons for more than 20 years until a computer data company took over its schedule-

Making it to Opening Day involves a mass of math to ensure that every team plays the right 162 games.

building in 2005. If the NFL has half a million possibilities, imagine the huge numbers created by 30 teams playing 162 games in two countries (the U.S. and Canada)! In fact, in 2014, the organizers of baseball decided to make it three and expand on growing international interest. In April 2014, the Dodgers and Diamondbacks opened the season in Australia! The Stephensons are probably enjoying retirement.

Do teams and leagues need math? The

answer is as clear as 2 + 2: every single day in almost every single way.

TEXT-DEPENDENT QUESTIONS

1. What is one way that teams are responding to the growth of analytics?

2. For what type of games do teams use dynamic pricing?

3. What team got some help from fans in its 2014 draft?

RESEARCH PROJECTS

Pretend you were asked to help your favorite team draft new players. What sort of statistics would you look at? How would you research those players? Look ahead to your team's next draft and pick five players you think they should draft. (Then let the team know; they might appreciate the help!)

CHAPTER 4

GEAR FOR ALL

MATH AND SPORTS ARE CLEARLY LINKED, from the stats the players amass to the formulas that determine how their gear moves. For both pros and amateurs alike, turning the power of math into something they can use is where STEM really comes into play, if you'll pardon the pun. The math and science determine the principles that will make a product work. The engineers design gear that athletes, coaches, and others can use. And the result is technology unlike anything seen before.

Without the fundamental base of math and science, however, the gear would just be paperweights.

Thanks to wearable tech, athletes can now get their stats on the go.

Go, Go Gear!

In the growing field of wearable tech, the science of exercise **physiology** meets math and engineering. Athletes of all sorts are wearing wristbands, vests, or shoe inserts that gather data during workouts. The calculators in the devices then work out how many calories have been burned or how much distance has been traveled.

The FitBit is a combination of calculator and trainer. The sensors on the small clip-like device keep track of all your movements through the day and calculate how far you've traveled, how fast, and how much exercise you got. It also provides a constant stream of digital advice, showing how many more steps you need to reach a goal or to "praise" you

WORDS TO UNDERSTAND

physiology a branch of science that deals with living bodies and their parts and systems

Wearable devices link wirelessly to apps to help improve performance.

for success achieved. It also uploads the information to a mobile app so that you have an ongoing digital story of your movements.

The Nike+ FuelBand performs similar functions, but in a wristband complete with a nifty digital readout of various data.

Some of the bands connect to national chains of sports clubs or gyms so users can keep track of their workouts with the help of a computer system. Other bands track the lack of movement and send a signal when it's time to get up from the office chair and move around.

Burn, Calories, Burn

Here is a chart that shows approximately how many calories an average adult burns off during 60 minutes of exercise in various events. The wearable tech devices calculate this automatically, but you can plan ahead to create a workout target.

Exercise	Calories Burned
Basketball game	544
Belly dancing	306
Jogging	612
Martial arts	599
Shoveling snow	422
Swimming laps	476
Ultimate Frisbee	544
Walking (moderate speed)	225

Losing weight and getting in shape is basically a math question. You want to take in fewer calories than you burn off. Wearing these devices can help you and any athlete get the information needed to reach fitness goals.

Help from the Heavens

G EOMETRY IS A PART OF THE MATH WORLD THAT has numerous applications in sports. In late 2013, fans around the world got a close-up look at geometry in action during the America's Cup races. The super high-tech boats all had numerous sensors on board that

SportVision used its innovative tech to calculate and display real-time racing information.

GATE
3

NZL-B
BOAT SPEED
7.6kts

FRA-P
BOAT SPEED
14.7kts

tracked their position to within a few feet. Using satellites connected to the global positioning system (GPS), the sensors calculated the current and future tracks of the boats as they moved over the water. Those calculations were translated into graphics that showed the TV audience what was going on.

Yacht racing is a tough sport to watch on TV. There are no real "yard markers" or field boundaries visible on the heaving water. The graphics, created by a constant series of high-level calculations, pre-

sented the action in real-time in a way that even newbies to the sport could understand. Ratings were way up over previous America's Cup telecasts, thanks in large part to the science and tech behind the information viewers got.

The racers themselves need to be math experts, however. They use computers on board, but also must have a deep understanding of

Few sports use math as deeply as high-end yacht racing, which depends on geometry and even trigonometry.

Math shows the way, but during a race, a skipper doesn't have much time to focus when he's sailing at more than 60 miles per hour.

boat angles, wind speeds and directions, and sail arrangements. They must make decisions in an instant that can mean victory or defeat. Before races, they study the charts and understand the geometry of the course so that it's second nature when the gun goes off.

It worked out well for the America-based Oracle team. Though it trailed 8 races to 1, Orcale reeled off eight consecutive victories to capture the Cup in one of the most thrilling series of races in the 163-year history of the event.

To Pit or Not to Pit

RACE CARS OF ALL SORTS NEED ONE THING TO KEEP moving: fuel. Well, they need a driver, too, but fuel makes the engines go. The cars can't finish the race on one tank of fuel; they need to return to the pits to get more. Deciding when to come in for fuel is one of the most important decisions a race team makes, and the team depends on math (and computers) to help them make it.

The math is pretty simple: If a car uses X gallons per mile and you know how many gallons are left, then how many more miles will the car go until it runs out? The tricky part is that the X changes throughout the race. A faster pace might burn fuel more quickly; a slow pace less so. An engine problem might eat up fuel. That's where the computers come in. Teams have them in action

Is it time to stop for gas? **NASCAR** teams look to math to tell them when it's the right time to fuel up.

from the first moments. The team constantly feeds its computers new data so that there is a running calculation of fuel usage and need. One interesting fact: NASCAR cars, for one example, do not have fuel gauges. The pit crew keeps track of the fuel by weight. Crew members can calculate how fast the fuel is used so they know how much is left.

From the highest levels of sports to the everyday jogger, people involved in athlet-

Formula 1 cars stop less often than in **NASCAR**, so every stop is crucial to success.

ics cannot escape the reach of math. The numbers are part of every physical activity, whether to show progress or to determine a winner. Let's hope that's you.

TEXT DEPENDENT QUESTIONS

1. Which activity discussed burns off the most calories?

2. How do NASCAR teams measure fuel?

3. What branch of math helps America's Cup boats find their way?

RESEARCH PROJECTS

Time to work out! Find an online calculator that shows how many calories are burned in five of your favorite ways to exercise. Also, look for everyday activities that burn calories, from vacuuming to raking leaves. Find some new ways to "feel the burn!"

WINNING . . . AND THE FUTURE

CHAPTER 5

WILL TOMORROW'S PITCHERS, fielders, and racers need advanced math degrees to succeed? Probably not, but the more that athletes and others understand how math plays a part in sports the better chance they'll have to bring home trophies.

As we've seen, math now plays a part in every aspect of sports. In the future, look for that trend to continue and deepen. Most of the advances will come behind the scenes, not on the fields of play. Team executives will dig deeper into "big data" to find other ways to improve their teams.

For the men and women who created this mathematical revolution—the fans with fast computers and curious minds—this "mainstreaming" of big data in sports comes with a price. They're not running the show anymore.

"The question," according to Colin Wyers of the stat-heavy Baseball Prospectus Web site, "is really whether or not the current Sabermetrics movement is going to be a part of

These players won thanks to hitting and pitching. But will math someday tell them where to pitch and how to hit?

[the future]. And if so, will they be on the side of the outsiders, or will they be the establishment being rebelled against?" Sabermetrics is aimed at baseball, but the question is true of just about every other team sport.

Some observers of this sports stats scene think that, in baseball at least, Sabermetrics has reached a new turning point. Writer Andrew Zimbalist said that the "low-hanging fruit has all been picked," meaning that the "easy" new stats are all in play now. What is next? What is the new way to take math and numbers and revolutionize sports again? Will the fans of 10 years from now look back on today's statheads as a bunch of rookies? Or will the game-changers in sports today be seen as pioneers?

The debate about the importance and usefulness of big data, math, and numbers in sports will go on. There remain big pockets of resistance among the old guard that still prefer the eyeball test over the spreadsheet. But they are now the outliers. Sports analytics is the present . . . and the future.

What does this mean for you? It might mean a job. More and more teams, leagues, agents, and corporations are turning to math- and stat-based graduates to bring their knowledge of data-gathering and analysis to their businesses.

And remember that MIT conference mentioned back on page 26? One of the 2014 topics was "From the Classroom to the Locker Room: Teaching the Next Generation of Sports Analysts." Is that going to be you?

If so, see you at the ballpark or the arena—and bring your laptop.

FURTHER RESOURCES

Books
Analytic Methods in Sports
By Thomas Severini (CRC Press, 2014)
Looking for a challenge? This textbook-like product dives deep into the math need to find answers to sports questions of all kinds.

The Math of the Game (Series)
By Shane Frederick (Sports Illustrated for Kids, 2011)
Ignore the "kids" part of the publisher's name: These are good books for understanding about stats in the major sports of baseball, basketball, football, and hockey.

Mathematics and Sports
Edited by Joseph Gallian (MAA, 2010)
This is a collection of articles and essays covering a wide range of sports-math topics, though some are written for a college-age or older audience.

Real World Math: Sports (Series)
By Cecilia Minden (Cherry Lake Publishing, 2014)
Another series that covers applications of math in a series of sports, this time including individual sports like swimming, running, and speed skating.

Web Sites
MIT Sloan Sports Conferences
http://www.sloansportsconference.com/
Watch videos and read papers presented at the country's top sports analytics conference.

SERIES GLOSSARY: WORDS TO UNDERSTAND

aerodynamic The science of how air moves and how objects move through it

applications In this case, ways of using information in a specific way to find answers

carbon fiber A material woven of carbon atoms that offers a wide range of high-strength and high-flexibility properties

cognitive training Software and hardware that trains the brain and the body's senses

fluid dynamics The science of how air or liquid moves over a surface

GPS: Global Positioning System Technology that bounces a signal off satellites to pinpoint the exact location of where the signal originated from

logistics The science of organizing large numbers of people, materials, or events

parabola A symmetrical curved path. In stadiums, a roof overhang can create a parabola by bouncing noise from below back down toward the field of play

prosthetics Devices that replace a missing human limb

prototype A model of a future product made to test design and engineering issues.

rehabilitation The process of returning to full physical ability through exercise

velocity Measurement of the speed of an object

ventilation The easy movement of air around or within a body or a system

INDEX

Photo Credits

Front cover: DollarPhotoClub/WavebreakmediaMicro
Interior Images: Courtesy of Sportvision & Americas Cup Event Authority: 52; Dreamstime.com: Upthebanner 6; Nejron 8; Alexander Dobre 11; Rob Corbett 12; Ottmar Winterleitner 15; Rob Blisset 16; Felix Miznoznikov 18; Pixattitude 20; Lawrence Weslowski Jr. 23, 55; Steven Cukrov 24; Courtesy MIT Sloan Sports Analytics Conference 27; Cao Hai 30; Rccster 32; Eric Broder Van Dyke 35; Yobro 10 36; Richard Kane 38, 40, 42; Aguina 45; Joshua Daniels 46; Martinmark 48; Aleksey Boldin 50; Arekmelang 51; Gustavo Fernandes 53; Blackkango 54; Sergei Bachlakov 56; Eduard Bonnin Turina 58; Photographerlondon 60. Joe Robbins: 29, 39
Backgrounds: Dreamstime.com/Shuttlecock (2)

About the Author

James Buckley Jr. has written more than 100 books on sports for young readers. He is a former editorial projects manager for *Sports Illustrated* and a senior editor at NFL Publishing, where he was on the team that started NFL.com. In 2012, he was the editor of *NFL Magazine*. His recent books include titles on baseball history, the Pro Football Hall of Fame, and even robots, along with biographies of Jesse Owens, Muhammad Ali, and Roberto Clemente. He is president of Shoreline Publishing Group and lives in Santa Barbara, California.